My Memories Journal

Created by Lynne Edwards & Meryl Adams
Published by Lynne Edwards
Mount Martha, Victoria, Australia
lynneedwardsauthor@gmail.com
Copyright 2024
All rights reserved. No portion of this book may be reproduced in any form without permission from the publisher except as permitted by US, UK and Australian copyright law.
ISBN: 978-0-9756516-2-9

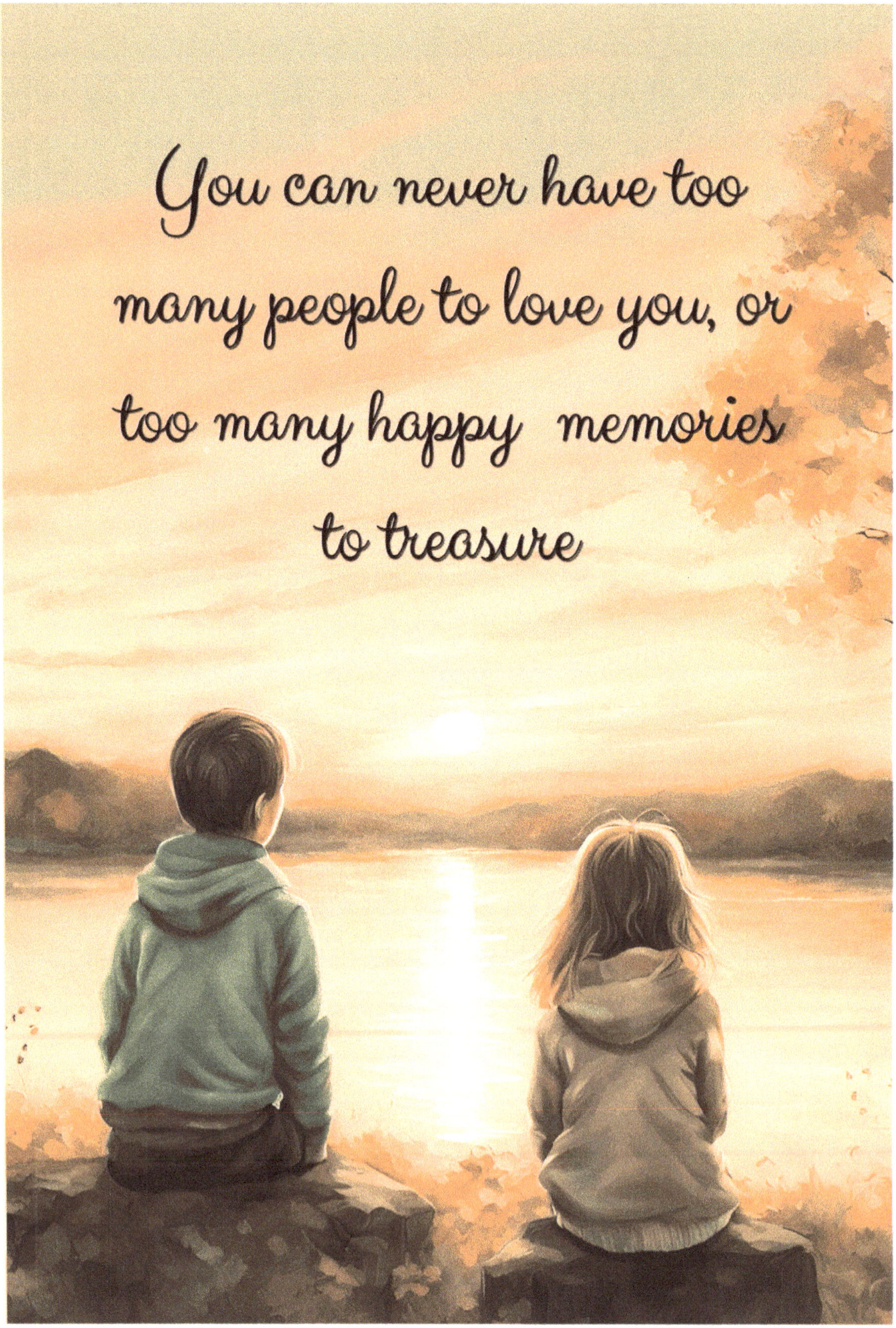
You can never have too
many people to love you, or
too many happy memories
to treasure

Contents

Page 3: Unique Me
Page 5: Hand & Footprints
Page 7: My Health
Page 8: Immunisation
Page 9: Look at me Grow
Page 11: My Hairstyles
Page 13: My Teeth
Page 15: My Firsts
Page 19: Growing Up
Page 27: Kinder and School Days
Page 37: Friendship
Page 43: Birthdays
Page 53: Christmas and/or other Special Times of the Year
Page 56: Favourite Things
Page 61: Memorable Quotes
Page 63: Milestones
Page 67: Holidays
Page 73: Special Occasions
Page 77: More Memories

Unique Me

Name:

Date of Birth:

Place of Birth:

Birth Weight:

Birth Length

Eye Colour:

Hair Colour:

Complexion:

I am Special!

This is Me!

 # Hand & Footprints

Unique every step of the way!

My Health

My important health details.

Allergies/Intolerances

Illnesses:

Procedures

Immunisation

I have been immunised against:

Date	Type

Notes:

Look at Me Grow

Date:	Age	Weight	Height
Date:			CM
Date:			CM
Date:			CM
Date:			CM
Date:			CM
Date:			CM
Date:			CM
Date:			CM
Date:			CM
Date:			CM
Date:			CM
Date:			CM
Date:			CM

Date:	Age	Weight	Height
Date:			
Date:			
Date:			
Date:			
Date:			
Date:			
Date:			
Date:			
Date:			
Date:			
Date:			
Date:			
Date:			
Date:			
Date:			

My Hairstyles

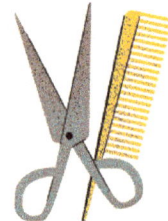

Curly, straight, long or short?

13

My Teeth

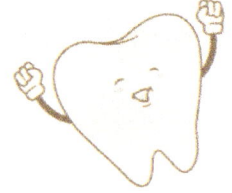
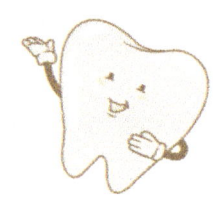

The journey of my smile.

Tooth Arrived **Tooth Fell Out**

_____ _____

_____ _____

_____ _____

_____ _____

_____ _____

_____ _____

_____ _____

_____ _____

_____ _____

_____ _____

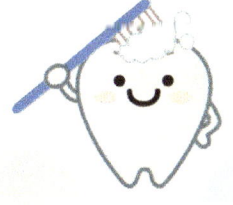

Tooth Arrived   Tooth Fell Out

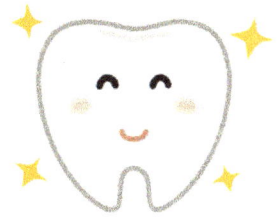

 # My Firsts

There's a first time for everything.

17

18

Growing Up

Pictures of me from small to tall.

24

25

Kinder & School Days

Friends, teachers, achievements, events and projects.

29

30

31

32

33

34

35

36

37

 # Friendship

Special friendships, connections and acts of kindness.

39

40

41

42

43

Birthdays

My birthday is the:

____ of _____

Special moments, surprises, gifts and activities.

49

50

51

52

53

Christmas and/or other Special Times of the Year

So many special occasions to remember.

My Favourite Things

Toys, colours, pets, songs, movies, activities.

59

60

61

Memorable Quotes

Funny and interesting things I've said, heard, or read.

 # Milestones

Achievements and significant events in my life.

 # Holidays

Time out with friends, family or with my amazing self.

70

71

72

73

Special Occasions

Special moments, surprises, gifts and activities.

76

 # More Memories

So many more things to not be forgotten.

80

81

83

84

www.ingramcontent.com/pod-product-compliance
Lightning Source LLC
Chambersburg PA
CBHW061400160426
42811CB00099B/1309